ALASKA
KESUGI RIDGE
Stephen Platt

www.leveretpublishing.com

Alaska: Kesugi Ridge
First published - December 2024
Published by Leveret Publishing
56 Covent Garden, Cambridge, CB1 2HR, UK

Bald Eagle (white-headed sea eagle)

ISBN 978-1-912460-06-9

ALASKA 2014

Day 1 Anchorage

Sunday 20 July 2014

I caught an early morning flight from Heathrow and, after changing in Frankfurt, I arrived at Ted Stevens International Airport in Anchorage on Sunday late morning after a 14-hour flight. I found my way to the Hilton Hotel. There was a street fair and summer festival in progress in the parking and park opposite the hotel and I wandered over and found a seat near the live music stage and sat in the warm sunshine listening to jazz.

Alaska is huge. Its name in Aleut is "Great Country". I had come for a conference and, despite the bears, planned to go walking on my own. I was excited. Alaska conjured up thoughts of gold prospectors and polar bears, the ice road to Prudhoe Bay and Denali, the highest mountain in North America. Alaska is the largest US state. It is separate from the rest of the United States and borders the Yukon in Canada to the east and to the west it is only 55 miles across the Bering Strait to Russia. Indigenous

Anchorage from Knick Arm of Cook Inlet

people have lived in Alaska for thousands of years and Russian fur traders began visiting from the mid 18th century. In 1867 William H. Seward, United States Secretary of State, negotiated the purchase of Alaska from Russia for $7.2 million (equivalent to $157 million in 2023). For a decade or so there was only a small community of settlers in Sitka and the purchase was widely known as .Seward's Folly. But in 1890 gold was

Map of the places I visited

discovered and that changed everything as prospectors poured in. By 1920 Alaska had produced over $6.5 trillion at 2023 prices.

Alaska was important during World War II. The Japanese captured a number of the Aleutian Islands and Unalaska, another island, was an important American base ferrying war planes to Russia as part of the Lend lease program. Oil was discovered in Prudhoe Bay in 1968 and the Trans-Alaskan pipeline, opened in 1977 led to an oil boom. Thanks to oil and gas, and to fishing and tourism, Alaska has a high per capita income. Interestingly it is one of the most irreligious states, the first to legalise recreational marijuana, and is known for its libertarian culture.

I was here to give a paper at an earthquake conference and I also planned to do Kesugi Ridge, a 30-mile, three day ridge walk just to the east of Denali. I must have read about it in a book about great walks of the world. Kesugi means the 'ancient one' in Dena'ina Athabaskan. According to Wikipedia, "This hike can be considered difficult because of the elevation gain, exposure to sudden changes in weather and of bear activity. At times the presence of bear forces the closure of the trail." This naturally gave me pause for thought. Although I'd done plenty of solo

Listening to jazz in the park soon after arriving

walks in Scotland and elsewhere I was anxious.

I got organised for the walk back in England. I would need to camp on the ridge because unlike hiking in Europe, there are no refuges. I had plenty of old camping gear but I felt I needed to get lightweight equipment. So I went on-line and did my research. I bought a Nordisk Danish tent and a Lightwave rucksack, each weighing less than a kilo. I got a Jetboil stove that integrated the pan with the burner and gas cannister into a single unit. And I bought new Meindl leather boots. The rest of the gear I had already.

There is a Summer Solstice fair every year. There were dozens of brightly coloured stalls in Buttress Park selling all manner of fast food and lots of local artists selling their paintings, carvings and jewelry. There were noisy children's rides and hundreds of people milling around enjoying themselves. I found it all a bit over-whelming, being tired and jet-lagged from the long journey. So I wandered through the site and north towards the river and along the Ship Creek Trail. There were people on the foot bridge looking down into the creek at the Scenic Overlook and I went to join them. They were watching the salmon running upstream to spawn. There were fishermen wading in shallow river and I could see the salmon,

Summer fete

Stalls at summer fete

Salmon running Ship Creek

silver and pink flashes of energy in the sparkling water. The hundreds of Chinook King Salmon looked huge in the shallow pools, but somehow they managed to find a way through. They go through an amazing transformation from sleek silver greeny blue of Pacific Ocean fish, to pink and deep red as they enter the river to spawn. I was entranced and stopped there till it was time to go and eat and get to bed.

Main Street 4th Avenue

Day 2 Anchorage

Monday 21 July 2014

I ventured forth to explore down-town. My first stop was the Alaska Public Lands Information Centre in the Federal Building on 4th Avenue just around the corner from my hotel. A stuffed muskox caught my fancy. I thought they would be much bigger and more bovine. It seems they are more closely related to sheep and goats than cows or oxen. Their thick coats mean they can survive the Arctic winter. Their name in in Inuktitu is "bearded one" and their wool is highly prized.

4th Avenue is the main shopping street – Big Ray's The Alaskan Outfitter, Luck Grocery and Deli, Rapper Jacks Trading Post, the Alaskan Fur Gallery, the Hard Rock Cafe, cocktail bars, tour agencies, gift shops and the Federal Building and Courthouse. I bought a couple of things I needed for my walk in the Army and Navy Surplus store and the Downtown Bike shop. I also wanted to get some advice and guidance from fellow climbers.

Muskox in the Land Information Centre

I was nervous at the thought of meeting a bear with cubs. I'd read that bear canisters aren't required but were strongly recommended. So I walked down L Street a couple of miles to the Anchorage Mountaineering and Hiking store on Spenard Road.

The guys in there were friendly and helpful but didn't set my mind at rest. They asked if I had a gun. I said no. Then you'll need a pepper spray, they said. Just remember don't run; a grizzly can run much faster than you. And make sure they know you're there. The last thing you want to do is come on a mother and cubs unexpectedly. I dithered about buying the pepper spray. Maybe it would enrage the bear and make it more likely to attack or maybe the wind would blow the pepper back into my own eyes. But they also told me about the hike – where to park and start the walk and where I could bail out half-way along if the weather turned bad. They said that I'd have to hitch to my car as it was too far to walk back along the road and that the weather seemed set fair for the next few days. I ended up buying a small Gerber pocketknife. It was very light and sharp. It wouldn't do much good in a bear fight but I needed a knife and it made me feel better.

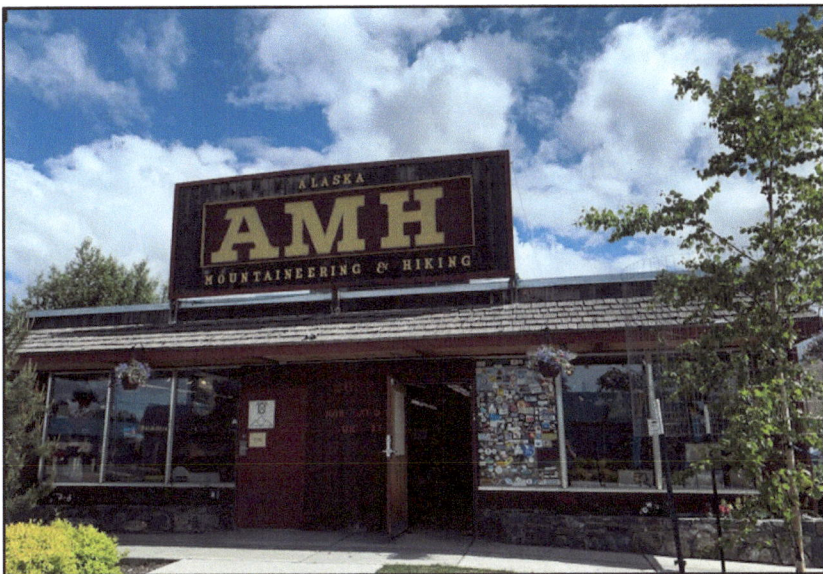

Alaska Mountaineering and Hiking shop

Timber houses in Anchorage

I walked back through the Anchorage suburbs taking photos of timber houses that took my fancy. Away from the town centre the city is green at this time of the year and homes are large, detached houses, many of which are timber clad. I reached the sea and looked out across the bay towards Fire Island. This is the Knik Arm and a long way to the open ocean from here and the coastline is complex, which must have made communications tricky in the past. I walked back along the Tony Knowles Coastal Trail.

That evening I joined Emily for dinner at the Crush Bistro on G Street just four minutes from our hotel. I felt adventurous and ordered king crab. The plate, when it arrived was a surprise. There was a neat ball of rice, a small pile of julienne vegetables and three very long pink crab legs from which one had to scrape out the meat. Emily had halibut and green fettucine.

Dinner with Emily

Maps of 1964 Alaska Earthquake (Mw 9.2)

Day 3 Earthquake Conference

Tuesday 22 July 2014

Today is the first day of the earthquake conference and the first session was about the Alaska Earthquake and Tsunami. This was a mega disaster on Good Friday in 1964 and is the most powerful ever recorded in North America. Anchorage suffered the most damage and many homes and commercial buildings were destroyed and sidewalks, bridges, sewers water mains and electrical systems were severely damaged. This explains why all the houses and buildings look so new. Places near Kodiak were raised by 30 feet (9 m) and areas around Girdwood and Portage on Turnagain Arm where I planned to go after Kesugi ridge, dropped 8 feet (2.4 m). Girdwood was relocated inland and Portage was abandoned. The Seward Highway had to be raised to get it above the new high tide. Coastal towns on the Kenai Peninsula like Whittier, where I also intended to visit, were heavily damaged.

1964 Earthquake estruction on main street

The quake was caused by tectonic plate action. Alaska is where the Pacific plate subducts or pushes beneath the North American plate. Two types of tsunami followed the shaking. The initial tectonic tsunami was followed by a series of tsunamis caused by undersea landslides. And it was these that caused the tsunami damage. 131 people died – nine as a result of the earthquake and 122 from subsequent tsunami.

Anchorage appointed a team of 40 scientists to assess the damage and guide the recovery. Despite conflict with downtown business owners who wanted to rebuild immediately the team produced their report in a little over a month and buildings were built back better. the U.S. Army Corps of Engineers led the effort to rebuild roads, clear debris, and establish new townsites for communities that had been completely destroyed, at a cost of $110 million

Emily and I invited friends to join us for dinner at the Crush Bistro. Maki, Hitomi and Joshua Macabuag had been with us both on the EEFIT mission to Japan the previous year. We went to investigate the recovery after the 2011 Great East Japan Earthquake. This was the largest earthquake ever recorded in Japan and the most expensive natural disaster ever worldwide.

Dinner with colleagues

My job had been to report on planning; for example, whether people living in villages with declining populations or in high risk locations might be relocated. One of the things I discovered was how risk averse elderly Japanese people are, how resistant to moving and how they demanded massive sea walls be built to protect them in the future. From what I'd read I imagined that people in Alaska would be much more cavalier and tolerant of risk. The average age of the population is much lower in Alaska, but it was more to do with a spirit of independence that's ingrained in Americans and pronounced in Alaska.

Field survey 2011 Tohoku Earthquake and Tsunami

Day 4 Conference paper

Today I give my paper. I'm on after lunch at 1.30. Unfortunately Emily is giving her paper about the earthquake consequences database at the same time as I'm speaking. My talk described how we used a scenario planning game with teams of disaster managers in Bishkek, Kyrgyzstan and Izmir, Turkey. The idea was to explore how managers made decisions after a major disaster and how we might provide information at different stages of recovery. The game worked well but we the managers had difficulty in using the information. The pace of events and the need to make decisions under time pressure meant people couldn't wait. They made decisions based on experience, gut reaction or standard ways of doing things. Daniel Kahneman, the Nobel prize-winning economist calls this kind of instinctive decision making "thinking fast". The sort of information we could provide favours reflective "slow thinking". To me, this suggested that two types of

SENSUM Game with civil defence crisis managers Bishkek, Kazakhstan

18

Polar and Brown bear in the lobby of the Hilton Hotel

teams need to be appointed to manage catastrophes. We need civil defence personnel who can make swift effective decisions to manage the immediate response and a separate team to plan recovery and reconstruction.

Later Emily and I met David Wald a seismologist from the U.S. Geological Survey. Emily had been working with him on a project called Pager. The Pager system provided fatality and loss estimates following significant earthquakes with 24 hours of an event. We wanted to talk to him about who used the one-page reports and how useful they were. He was very friendly but I got the impression that he wasn't interested in a user survey like this. I think he felt that the system was as good as it could get and he wasn't going to risk finding out that it wasn't as well used or as useful as he supposed.

Flattop Mountain (1,070m)

Day 5 Flattop Mountain 3,510 feet (1,070 m)

Thursday 24 July 2014

Emily left today, and I'm staying on to go walking. Today I plan to climb Flattop Mountain. Flattop is in Chugach State Park just east of urban Anchorage and is the most climbed mountain in the state. It's close to Anchorage, can be climbed in an afternoon, and there is a shuttle bus from near my hotel to the trailhead. The shuttle left at midday and drove us the 16 miles to the Glen Alps trailhead. The drover told us we had to get back by 4pm and would wait there for us.

The climb, only a three-mile round trip with an ascent of 1,300 feet, would be a good introduction to walking the trails in Alaska. I left the others from the bus and began on the earth path around Blueberry Loop. This walking was easy the weather was fine and it was good to be out. Where it steepened there were steps constructed from railroad ties and stepping up got hard on the knees and thighs. The last stretch to the

Summit of Flattop looking back towards Anchorage

summit is a rocky scramble. There were views back to the city and the ocean and looking southeast along the ridge there were views of O'Malley Peak and Powerline Pass. I got back in good time and had time to shower and rest before going out to an evening at the Alaska Native Heritage Centre.

It was interesting. Different indigenous cultures in Alaska were represented at "village" sites on the paths around the pond, rather like a trade show. The hosts on each stand were available to provide information and answer questions but I found it all rather off-putting and wished I'd come with someone to help overcome my shyness. The people hosting the stands were also reserved and withdrawn and it wasn't clear that they wanted to be here. I found it artificial, and somewhat embarrassing and almost wished I hadn't come.

There were various birds of prey including a pair of magnificent bald eagles. A part subterranean dwelling of driftwood, whale bone and turf with seal oil lamps for lighting and heating showed how people survived the cold winters. The extreme Artic climate was no barrier to life but rather provided a bounty of mammals, birds, fish and fruits to support a

Summit of Flattop looking SW into Chuguch Mountains

Alaska Native Heritage Centre

Traditional dance

rich way of life until whalers arrived in the 1850's bringing alcohol and disease. Subsistence hunting is now threatened by intense competition from sport hunting and commercial fishing.

Food – American hamburgers, BBQ fare and beer and I began to feel better! We were ushered into the open auditorium to performances of traditional dances depicting local animals and birds and telling stories about the land and historical events which I much enjoyed because the performers seemed to be enjoying themselves.

Later, I discovered that there are five main regional groupings: Iñupiaq in the Arctic; Athabascan in the interior; Yup'ik in the west, Aleut and Alutiiq in the southwest and Eyak, Haida, Tsimshian, and Tlingit in the southeast. However, looking at maps of native language groups, the picture seemed much more complex than this and the central Athabascan region seemed subdivided into at least nine or ten language groups. Interestingly, in the Dena'ina and other native speech the word for language also means people or ethnic group. No wonder I was confused at the Heritage Centre gathering.

It is thought that ancestors of Native Alaskans migrated into the area

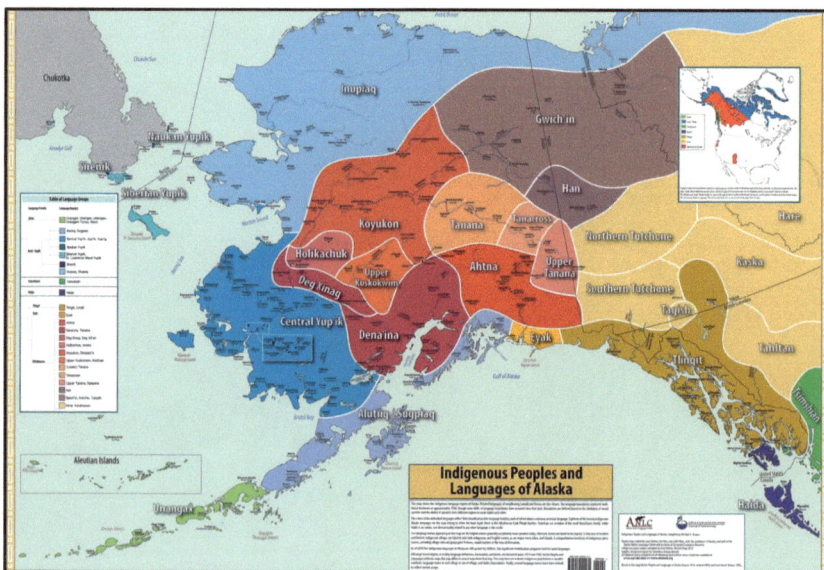

Indigenous Peoples and Languages

thousands of years ago, in distinct waves. Some are descendants of the third wave of migration, in which people settled across the northern part of North America. Genetic studies show that they never migrated to southern areas and are not closely related to native peoples in South America.

The bays between the Chugach and Talkeetna Mountains provided abundant fishing, hunting, and gathering grounds. Anchorage is within the traditional homelands of the Dena'ina Athabascan people and the native people of Knik Arm of Anchorage are members of the Eydlughet and K'enakatnu tribes. Many place names in Anchorage are historically significant in Dena'ina life. The construction of the Alaska railroad 1914-23 from Seward in the south to Fairbanks and the subsequent development of Anchorage significantly disrupted native life, and the 1918 influenza epidemic devastated local Dena'ina communities.

Athabascan People

Boy leaping outside reconstruction of a winter lodge

Day 6 Kesugi Ridge: Little Coal Creek

Friday 25 July 2014 Drive 250 miles; walk 4 miles ascend 1750 feet

Today is the last day of the conference and there are a couple of talks of tsunami social sence research I want to attend before heading off north. I've arranged to collect a car hire at 1.30 as soon as the conference finishes and head off north to Kesugi Ridge. I'm anxious. I have to pack and change and leave my big case at the hotel before walking to the Downtown Transit Centre and catching a bus to the airport to collect the car before driving 250 miles to Denali and then climbing 2000 feet to the ridge without running into a bear or two. I feel I may have bitten off more than I can chew and have a nagging presentiment that something is going to go wrong.

The Old Glen Highway north passes through the usual low density bill-boarded out of town development and through Chugiak. Development thins and the road narrows to single lane on the downhill stretches. I

Old Glen Highway north

switch to the Parks Highway, a smooth fast two-lane road but I keep to the speed limits of 55 and 65 mph. Pine forests line the route with occasional views of the mountains. The weather is good, it doesn't really get dark at this time of the year so I relax and resign myself to the four or five hour drive. I cross the Kwik River with great views of snow-covered mountains and then Reflections Lake. This is a big country and I'm feeling both excited and a little daunted.

I pass through the lake township of Wasilla. Half the cars on the road are utility vehicles and my tiny hire car seems very small alongside them on the three-lane highway through town. Out of town the road narrows to a single lane highway but there isn't much traffic and I make good progress. It's been surprisingly flat till now. Perhaps I was expecting more hills. The road goes on and on. Signs advertise views of Denali, but I can't see the mountains from the road and the drive is getting boring. I pass Sheep Creek Lodge, a fine old timber building and various camping grounds and RV parking areas.

At Talkeetna I pulled in at the Walter Harper Ranger Station. The rangers were friendly and encouraging but again they put the fear of god

Walter Harper Ranger Station at Talkeetna

into me by impressing the dangers of bear attacks, how it would be impossible to outrun a bear. Bears can reach speeds of 35-40 miles an hour and see you as prey if you run. They asked me if I had a gun or a pepper cannister. They told me that grizzlies are apex predators and if attacked by a grizzly bear you could play dead. But not with a black bear, you should fight back. They explained that it was most important not to attract bears to my tent while I slept. They insisted I take a large thick plastic barrel to store my food and anything else with a smell, like toothpaste, at night. I should imagine a triangle the points of which were 50 metres apart. My tent should be at one apex, where I cooked at another and finally the barrel at the third. The barrel was heavy and bulky with a screw top lid. The idea was that it would be indestructible and would roll if leapt on by a bear. I figured with a bit of jiggling I could strap it to the top of my rucksack. They wished me luck and I set off again. Despite the hassle of having to lug the barrel I was glad I called in and told them what I was doing and that I'd check back in with them on my way back when I'd, hopefully, finished the walk.

Grizzly bear fishing

I crossed the mighty Susitna River and headed north. I finally began to feel I was getting there, passing Troublesome Creek and Byers Lake. There were few other cars on the road and the land felt empty and a little hostile. There was a small brown sign to Little Coal Creek and a pull-in where I could leave the car and no sign of a path. I parked up and put on my boots, shouldered my heavy pack and set off on the four mile climb to the ridge. The path was flat at first and then began to ascend through trees and then thick scrub. I was nervous about running into a bear, and as the rangers had told me, I shouted " Bear", "Bear", every few minutes, expecting a huge brown mother bear to emerge from the undergrowth at every turn in the path. Finally after a couple of hours steady climbing the vegetation began to thin, there were spectacular views across the Chulitna valley towards cloud covered Mount Eldridge and Mount Deception and the Eldridge Glacier.

I pass a stone cairn and reach a grassy shoulder under Indian Mountain and decide this will make a good camp site. It is exposed but the weather is fine and I pitch the tent on a level patch and unroll the Thermarest and my sleeping bag. My meal is freeze-dried Adventure Food pasta Bolognese

Little Coal Creek Trail in the late evening

Cairn below Indian Mountain

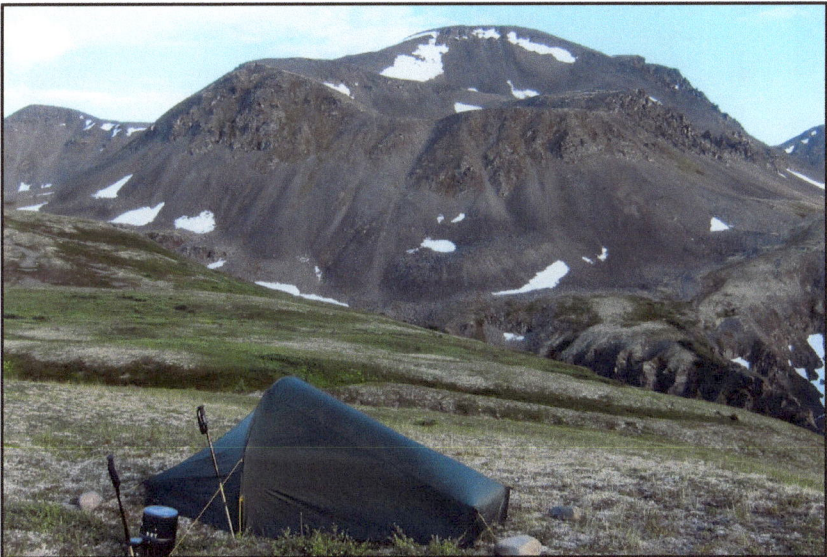

First night's camp

I'd bought in Anchorage. I follow the ranger's advice and cook away from the tent and site the barrel some way away. Although there are no sign of bear and I reason any bear is likely to be lower down on the creeks catching salmon I don't want to take any chances.

I lay in bed thinking about bears. Avoiding an encounter that could lead to an attack was clearly the best strategy. But how? Not surprising a bear seemed most important. Most bears, I'd been told, will avoid humans if they hear them coming. If you meet a bear on the path, it would be important to remain calm and still and to talk quietly to help the bear identify you as human and not prey. I'd been told it might come closer or stand on its hind legs to get a better look. This is curiosity, rather threatening behaviour and they usually just want to be left alone. I began to feel more relaxed. Now I was on the ridge I could see long distances. It was the kind of mountain terrain I was used to and felt at home in. So I lay back in my sleeping bag, pulled my mask over my eyes and went to sleep.

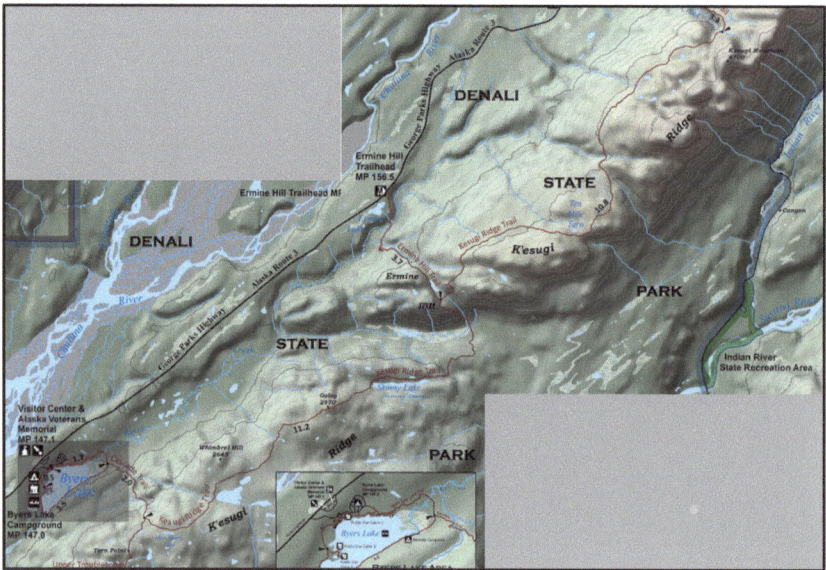

Map of Kesugi Ridge route (28 miles)

Day 7 Kesugi Ridge North: Little Coal Creek to Golog Mountain

Saturday 26 July 2014 (18 miles)

I was awake early the next morning and set off before seven. The faint trail headed down to the creek before climbing up a shoulder to reach the main ridge. I stopped at the creek and got out my Jetboil stove and made tea soon after ten. The walking was easy and there were good views of the braided River Chulitna and the nearby foothills of the Alaska Range and tantalising glimpses of the big mountains through cloud cover. It was a pity not being able to see Denali but given what I'd read about the possibility of bad weather, I was just glad it was warm and dry.

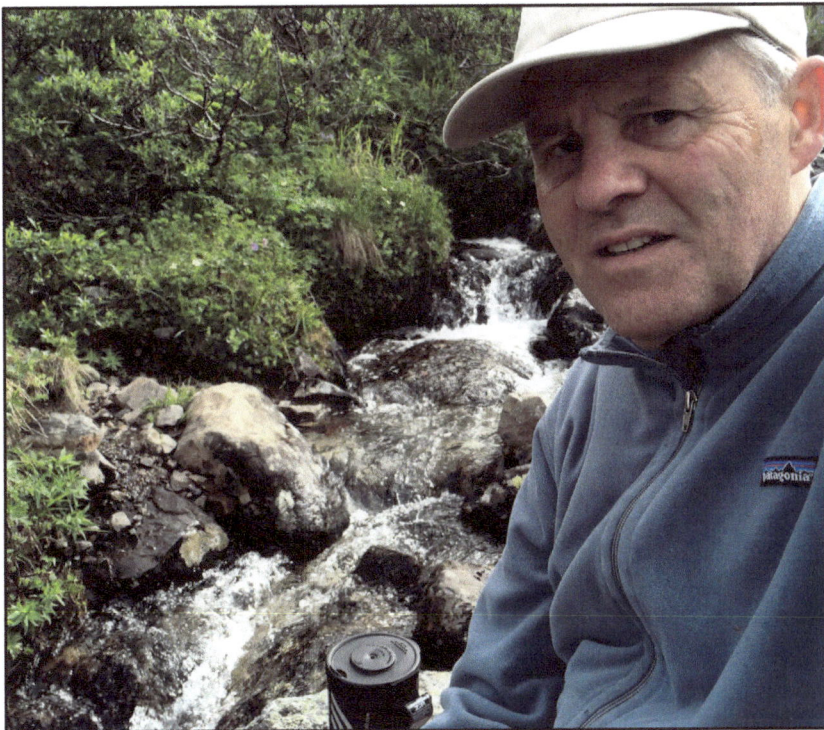

Brewing up by a babbling brook

Above the tree line this far north the land is known as tundra. Yet it seemed familiar and not unlike the tops in the Lakes or Scotland. I come upon a cascading stream like a winding staircase. There are small tarns and the ground is damper here and there were lots of wildflowers – yellow Nodding Arnica, pink Meadow Bistort looking like ground orchids, purple Wooly Cranesbill and pale blue Mountain Harebell. I reach a wide pass at 8-mile divide, and pass under Stonehenge Hill, the ground littered with boulders. It is easy to see why there are so many cairns.

After five hours of delightful undulating ridge I reached the dome of Ermine Hill and the saddle where the Ermine Hill Trail turns off. You can get back to the road here. It would be a good place to camp as there are flat patches of grass, but there's no water, so I press on. It's hot and dry , the path is shiny silver sand and there are strange grey and white contoured rocks on the skyline. It's quite a weird place.

The path begins to descend and it gets hotter out of the breeze on the ridge. It's now late afternoon and I've been walking seven hours and am beginning to feel tired. A group of four young people, boys and girls pass me with a big hello as I'm resting against a tree. I get my first views of

Tundra and small tarns

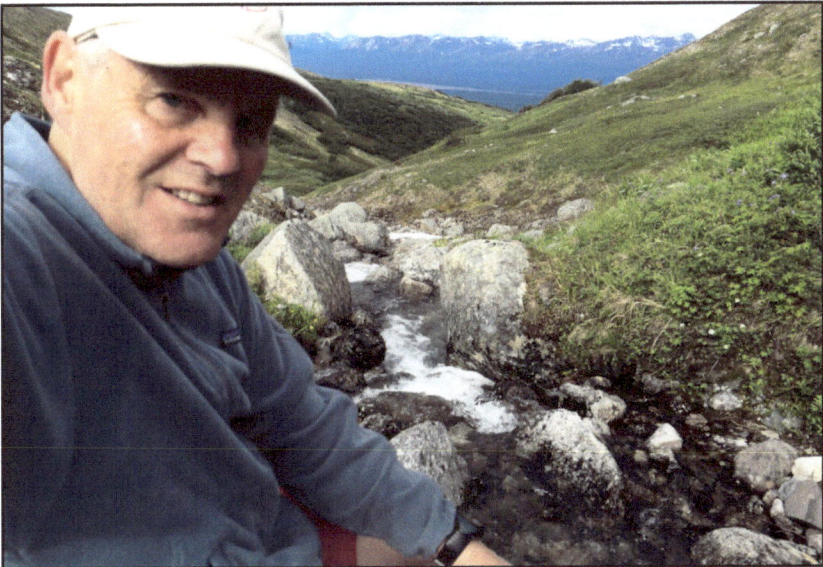

Rest stop by a stream

Strange rock formations at Ermine Hill

Ermine Hill trail

First view of Skinny Lake through dense undergrowth

Difficult traverse around Skinny Lake

Climbing ridge above the lake

Finally reach Golog Hill

Skinny Lake and the trail descends into thick undergrowth. Skinny Lake is a long narrow basin set amongst low granite ridges. The valley bottom here is heavily forested and I go back to my bear calling every minute or so.

It's hard going here. Not only do you have to push through the bush but the path is underwater and you are balancing on thick roots to avoid falling into your waist. I'd like to stop, but there is nowhere to camp and it's too hot and midgey. So I press on. The path steepens as it ascends Golog Hill. I'm tired, it's steep and I'm going slow, but I keep going and finally get to the top and look down at three small tarns and the two bright tents of the young party that passed me. I find a flat place and pitch my tent, fetch water and cook and then lean against a handy rock and contemplate the mountains to the west. it's a lovely spot. There is no problem with the light of course with 24 hours of day light, and I make camp on a lovely site with a panoramic view of distant Denali. There are patches of wild azalea, pink splashes of colour amidst mats of plait moss and crowberry. The rocks are patterned with grey lichen and there are swathes of delicate mountain avens, white petals with pale cream stamens. There are shouts and laughter from the tents below me as the girls strip off and go skinny-dipping.

Camp site on summit of Golog Hill

39

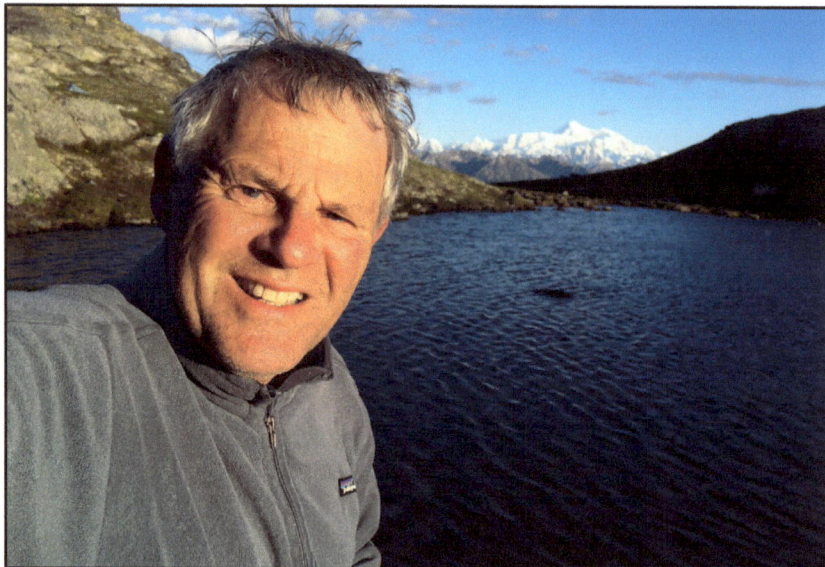

View of Denali in the early morning sunshine

Denali (6,190m)

Cairns on the ridge

Day 8 Kesugi Ridge South: Golog to Byers Lake

Sunday 27 July 2014 (8 miles)

I get a good night's sleep and wake early and set off before the others are stirring. For some reason I want to stay ahead of them today. I'm feeling good, refreshed after a good night's sleep, and the day has dawned clear and there are marvellous views of snow-covered Denali. It's so much bigger than anything else and quite dwarfs the adjacent mountains.

It's pleasant walking the final stretch. The rolling tundra is a close cropped green sward with occasional dwarf pines. The skyline is dotted with the sculptural forms of beautifully made granite cairns constructed I imagine for pleasure rather than necessity, since it would be difficult to lose one's way here even in cloud or mist. I stop for a break at a pretty stream and after more ridgeway catch my first view of Byers Lake.

First glimpse of Byers Lake

Byers Lake is where I plan to get back to the road. It's still early, only 10 o'clock, since I made an early start at six and I contemplate carrying on to the next trail head at Troublesome Creek. But the rangers have warned me that bears will be fishing there and I may run into a mother with cubs. So I take the path to Byers Lake which descends fairly steeply 2,000 feet down the Cascade Trail to the suspension bridge over Byers Creek. There are pretty stands of Twisted Stalk Claspleaf, golden bell flowers, like baubles on a Christmas tree, that might tinkle if you shook them.

I skirt round the north side of the lake and finally reach the road at the Alaska Veterans Visitor Centre. It's 17-18 miles back along the highway to Little Coal Creek, so I hitch. I soon get a lift with a friendly couple going to Cantwell who drop me back at my car. It's still early and I have plenty of time to drive back to Anchorage. I stop at the Ranger station at Talkeetna to drop off the barrel and tell them I'd made it back safely.

I take the coastal Seward Highway to Portage and Whittier. the only way to access this tiny coastal town by car from Anchorage is through a one-way tunnel. Whittier is wet and is known as "The Strangest Town in Alaska".

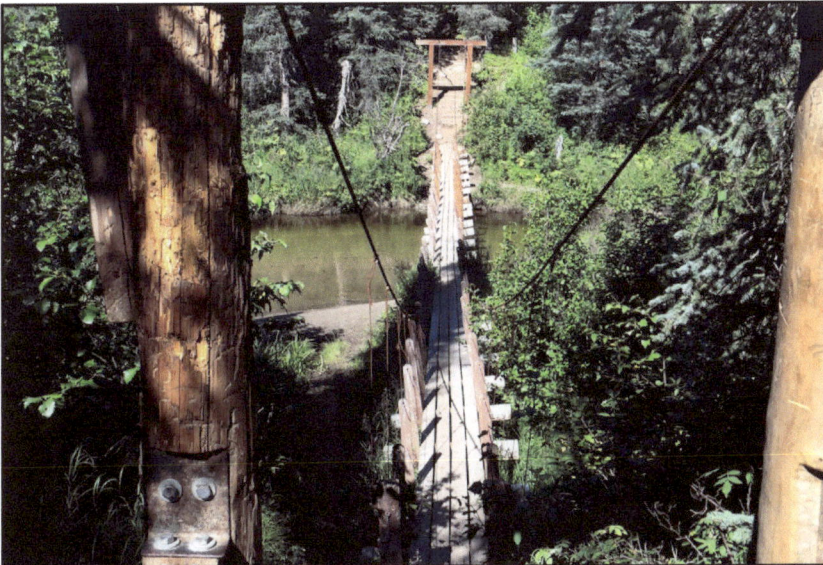

Suspension Bridge across Byers Creek

Day 9 Whittier, Portage and Crow Pass

Monday 28 July 2014

Whittier is strategically placed at the head of Prince William Sound and was once on the portage route of native peoples of the Chugach region along the Portage Creek and Portage and Burns Glaciers. The portage was later used by explorers and prospectors that avoided going round Kenai Peninsula. By 1939 the route became unusable as the glaciers retreated. During WW2 the U.S. Army built a military base and constructed the Anton Anderson rail tunnel. In 2000 this was converted to a bi-modal road and rail tunnel and Whittier took off as a tourist hub for cruise liners. It's quite a surreal experience driving through the tunnel. At 2.5 miles long it's the longest tunnel in America.

I spent the night at June's Whittier Condo on the top floor of an amazing multi-story apartment block like something from the Soviet Union. It's the only place to stay. The 14-story Begich Towers was built during the

Whiiter and cruise ship

Cold War 1953-57 by the US Army Corps of Engineers and used by the army till the early sixties. Three-quarters of the residents of Whittier live in the building as a condominium. The Condo got four stars on Booking.com but apart from the view it wasn't that great. It felt institutional, it wasn't that clean and I was cold that night. I woke early to a grey day. The port from my apartment window looks bleak. Breakfast was a stale sesame bagel in the fridge.

Portage tunnel for both cars and trains

I got away early. The trailhead for Portage pass is only five minutes by car, just past the tiny Whittier airport. The first 700 feet of the trail were quite steep, there was thick undergrowth of alders and this was obviously bear country. But by the third day of my Kesugi walk I had been looking forward to seeing a bear and was no longer that frightened. It's only five miles there and back. At the top there are great view of Portage Glacier and back to Whittier. The yellow wild raspberries and red elderberry are in fruit and I gorge myself. I continue down the path past the Great Divide Lake to Portage Lake.

Back through the tunnel and I can view Portage Lake and the glaciers from the west side of the divide. I park a few hundred yards after the tunnel entrance and walk down to the shoreline. There are blocks of ice that have carved off from the glacier are floating in the water. A hundred years ago this glacier filled the whole valley. There are now five fast diminishing ice sheets. Nevertheless it is still most impressive.

Next stop Crow Pass. Crow Pass is part of the thousand-mile Iditarod Seward to Nome Trail. From the Seward Highway you drive through the new town of Girdwood past the ski lodges and park at Milk Creek, Mile

Portage Pass trail

Portage Glacier much reduced in size

Portage Lake with floating blocks of ice

7.1 on Crow Creek Road. The path is well made at first, climbing through pine woods and I cross the creek by a board walk bridge and the path runs parallel with the creek for a while. Two miles into the walk, at the Monarch mine, there are signs of mine workings – a boiler tank, gear box and pair of pulley wheels. The silver braids of mountain streams brimming with meltwater pour over stone slabs and cascade down, swelling Crow Creek. At Crystal Lake there is an A-frame cabin, but it's all locked up and there's no-one about. Steeper uphill climbing and I reach Crow Pass after four miles. Here there are splendid views of a much diminished Raven Glacier and Eagle River. I halt at the col for a short while and admire the scene. There are patches of wild flowers – blue for-get-me-nots, punk Wood Sorrel and pale Stickwort. I go a little way down Raven Gorge towards the river, but don't continue since it's another eighteen miles to the Rapids Camp trailhead and there is no car or transport waiting for me there. Time to drive back to Anchorage and catch my plane.

I was congratulating myself on a successful trip. I hadn't crashed the car, got lost or tangled with a bear, but I still had that nagging feeling. I had to collect my suitcase from the hotel, change and repack, ditch the car and

Ancient Scots Pine

48

Pine woods on approach to Crow Pass

Abandoned mine machinery

Streams feeding Eagle River

A-frame hut by the side of Crystal Lake

Crow Pass (3,642ft)

Raven Glacier

Eagle River

check in. I had plenty of time, but I'm always anxious before going to catch a plane or train. So maybe that was all it was. I drove round from the hotel to Buttress Park and opened the suitcase to repack and change out of walking clothes and to my horror I couldn't find my little black knapsack with my notebook and laptop. I was sure I'd put it inside the suitcase. Or was I, I couldn't remember.

I need to go back and check if it's still in left luggage. What's the time; have I got enough time. It's not at the hotel. The manager is most solicitous. But it doesn't make sense. Why would anyone go in my suitcase and steal a knapsack? I was in a fluster; fear of missing my flight fighting with my intense desire not to lose my notebook and laptop. To the airport, deliver the car and check in and sit on the plane rueing the loss.

I was able to claim on my firm's insurance and replace the laptop and other stuff. But my notebook had all my notes from my two trips to Iran plus this conference. I wrote a letter to the Anchorage Daily News offering a reward of $200 without any luck. A loss adjuster employed by the Hilton Hotel rang me. I explained I was insured and so there was no monetary loss, just my precious notes. He offered my $500 which I thought was most generous.

The punch line is that thinking about it now 10 years later as I'm writing this journal I have a memory of wearing it on my front as I walked to the Transit Terminal in Anchorage with my big pack on my back. I think I must have hidden the knapsack in the car in the well where the spare wheel was stored.

www.ingramcontent.com/pod-product-compliance
Lightning Source LLC
Chambersburg PA
CBHW042130080426
42735CB00001B/39

*9 781912 460069 *